GOD LOVES YOU
Doodle King

A Messenger

DORRANCE
PUBLISHING CO
EST 1920
PITTSBURGH, PENNSYLVANIA 15238

Dorrance Publishing Co
585 Alpha Drive
Suite 103
Pittsburgh, PA 15238
Visit our website at *www.dorrancebookstore.com*

ISBN: 979-8-8860-4199-6
eISBN: 979-8-8860-4855-1

GOD LOVES YOU CAMPAIGN

Narration

It was not until my early sixties that I truly found and embraced the love of Jesus. I grew up having religion forced-fed to me and raised my own children in the same manner, because I thought that was the way. Well, my ignorance actually tore me apart from the church. And it wasn't until making a conscious accountability of my own spirituality that I was staring my redeemer face to face.

Early of 2020, I had jokingly told a dear friend that she should start a new website that just reflected her own thoughts on life. (She is quite a social butterfly.) Well, at the same time, God had been asking me to find a way to spread His love to all. And eventually I was the one that started a website fulfilling this request, and God Loves You Campaign was established.

Enjoy!

God loves you, and I do too!

Doodle King

God Loves You This Much:

You can't see anything, because my hands do not reach out to the ends of the universe. That's how much God loves each one of you...personally.

God's Love

Everything on this earth, under the earth, above earth...is God's Love. EVERYTHING!

Imagine, how does a small seed know to grow into a mighty tree? Or, how does a rock know how to form? Science can explain the physics behind it. But ultimately, who set this in motion?

What about the fascinating complicated intricate details of Man?

Science calls it DNA. But, ultimately, WHO started us in motion?

GOD'S LOVE.

GOD'S LOVE FOR HUMANITY

God loves all of us so much that He had sent His son Jesus to live amongst us. To bring salvation to all. By doing this, He fabricated a way so simple yet so unique that even wise men sought Him out.

God's gift of love to the world became known to shepherds, and kings, and yes, even to the unruly. And the birth of baby Jesus is still celebrated today, more than 2,000 years later.

Yes, it is understood that we don't know the actual day Christ was born. But we have interpreted and accepted it to be in the winter of December on the 25th. In fact, our whole calendar system, whether we are a believer or a non-believer, is based solely on the birth of Christ. So, even if you publicly denounce Jesus, you have accepted Him as your Lord and Savior just by accepting the calendar year for what it is.

This is God's way of expressing His love for all of us.

Happy Birthday, Jesus!

God loves you, and I do too!

GODS RENEWED LOVE

As I mature as a Christian follower of the teachings of Jesus Christ, I find many conflicts of how evil continues to try and take down the love of God by influencing the minds of humanity with altered truths of Christianity. One of the worst is how persuasive that Christmas is a pagan ritual.

It makes us question the very existence of God, and of Jesus Christ. If there were no God, then there would be no Jesus. Therefore, there would be no Christmas. It's not about the actual date Jesus was born into this world, but what He brought into this world.

For those who may not believe, I would like to share of the many miracles I have witnessed during the period of advent season leading up to Christmas Day. I've seen cold hearts soften, enemies lay down arms, generosity when all hope is lost, a kindred spirit for others, and anonymous love.

As we celebrate the advent season, let's reflect on the reason why. It is a time for us to be filled or renewed with God's Love, and the opportunity it presents for us to be able to share that unconditional love with others. Jesus came to us as a baby, to commoners, not to put himself above us, but to live among us. So that all shall experience a peace that has no understanding, hope for the oppressed, and unconditional love.

So, Christmas is a time of year to let ourselves go of the chains that restrict us and to feel, experience the happiness and joy of God's renewed, unconditional Love every year.

God bless you.
God loves you and I do too!
Merry Christmas and Feliz Navidad.

God's Throne

God sits at the Throne in Heaven. And Jesus is at His right. Like a king, He has earned this right because He IS King over all of us.

But it goes beyond this. He just doesn't sit there and watch over us as we go about our daily lives. You see, God is an active God. He participates right alongside us. He gets His hands wet. Walks in the muck and the mire with us. Stands next to us on the podium when we receive an award. His arm around us while we are grieving. Rejoices with us for our joy. When you let God in, He is with you always.

When you are hurt or grieving, do not blame God and ask "Why." What happens in your circle of life isn't because God wants you to be in pain or mental anguish. Rather, He wants you to know Love!

God bless you!

God loves you, and I do too!

God Rules by Love

God does not govern by rules and regulations. Nor by bylaws and preambles. Only the desire to love. Love of God. And love of neighbors.

He does not decide that He is a Baptist one day, and the next day a protestant, or Methodist. For God, it matters not whether you are Catholic, Mormon, Jewish, Evangelist, Agnostic, or Atheist. Only that you have the desire to love.

Jesus Christ is the church. It was built upon love. You are filled with the Holy Spirit. A gift given to you by God, who is love. And, because the Holy Spirit represents Jesus, so too, you are the church. And because the church was founded on love, so too, you are love.

God does not pick and choose who He decides to love, based on religion, denomination, set rules or laws. For He loves us all. And that's how He wants us to love.

He made us in His image, so how can we say no!

God bless you.

God loves you, and I do too.

God is Free

God does not charge money, like a performer, or goods. He offers Himself freely. To everyone.

He also gives us the freedom of choice. To believe, or not to believe. In Mark 12:17 Jesus says, render unto Caesar what is Ceasars. And to God what is God's.

When we tithe, we try not to let others know how much we put onto the plate. But tithing is not just about money. It is also how much time we put forth for the needs of others before ourselves. This, too, should be practiced anonymously.

As also when we pray. Pray in the confines of your own space, so as not to draw attention to others.

Because God is free, there is no reason for us to let others know how we accept Him.

For our true rewards will be in Heaven, not on Earth.

God bless you.

God loves you and I do too.

God Loves the Imperfect

If we had the perfect body, if we had the perfect life, what else could we want? Would we want God? Probably not. Because we would have everything we will ever need.

Well, in reality, God knows this, and that is why none of us are perfect. If we were, we would probably turn out to be a pansy. Not knowing how to handle situations as they arise.

Let me explain; but first let's reflect on the bible verse Job 13:15—Though he slay me, I will trust in him.

If God did not allow us to experience adversities, whether physical or life's situations in general, He knew we would not learn from these and would be weak minded. When we put our faith and trust in God, it makes our spirits stronger, especially during times of struggle. Without this faith and trust, our spirits would die. We must remain steadfast in the love for God, because He first loved us. And this is what keeps our spirits strong and alive.

So rest assured and be happy that you are filled with the joy of the Lord. And that it's okay to be imperfect. Because God loves you just as you are.

God bless you.

God loves you, and I do too.

God is in Control

As humanity evolves, we see growth in progress, technology, peace, compassion and love. But some pitfalls that came with this are wars, greed, selfishness, hatred, and control.

Every single natural living creature was created by one single entity. GOD! And God is Love. So each and everyone of us at the time of our conception was created through love. Everyone!

Through the existence of time, it has been the devil, Satan, to use whatever means possible at his disposal, including man, to try to overthrow the power of God. Because, like a child, he is having a tantrum for being chastised out of Heaven. And out of jealousy and revenge has been doing everything he can to get back in.

So, we can see how some go through life accepting Jesus Christ as our savior, and living a life of love. While others are obsessed with obtaining wealth, power, and total domination. To the point of entire annihilation of the human race. Because Satan is obsessed with stealing every soul from God. He does not care about humans, no matter how much he tries to sugar coat how well your life could be. All he wants is to take your soul, so that God can't have it.

So when you see man predicting, and moving, and making decisions of how humanity should progress forward, IT IS ALL FAKE!!!

It is the devil trying to make all this happen for his goals to obtain souls using all resources of man at his disposal.

This evil ring is huge...worldwide. In every part of countries, government, military, and religious sect.

They thrive on fear, complacency, ignorance.

But words of Jesus are given to us...believe, trust, faith, hope, love. Accept change for what it is. Never stop love of God. Always love your neighbor as yourself.

For only God knows when that day will come. Man has no control of this, regardless of how they try to manipulate the human mind into thinking otherwise.

Bottom line: follow God...not man.

God loves you, and I do too!

God's Love

Today's sermon is a perfect example of just how much love God has for you.

Jesus' unconditional love for Thomas, whom at first didn't believe it was the risen Jesus until Thomas actually saw Him.

For Jesus said, "Blessed are you that has seen and believe; more blessed are they that have not seen, and do believe."

Jesus loves everyone, whether you believe or not.

How wonderful to live in Gods never ending love!

God loves you, and I do too.

Church of God

Going to church is great. You get to be with church friends and families, and share a common belief in God as a community. And that's super great!

Now, each church, each religion has its own set of rules and policies that they feel is the best way to practice and worship in their faith. These policies don't always fit the individual's needs, and as an individual child of God, we should have the right to decide how we want to practice our faith, and not be shunned for it.

When Jesus Christ went about the lands, he preached of the good news and salvation. He was not interested in what church you belonged to. Rather, to show and to give love to all of humanity.

So, when you step into your church and enjoy the community fellowship offered, remember first, why you are there.

Because of God's almighty Love!

God loves you!

Understand God's Love

For everything that happens in this world, there is a reason.

It may not be for us to understand.

Whatever happens, good or bad, in our life, the real purpose is God's love.

We are so wrapped up in worldly thinking it is impossible for us to understand the true purpose of our circumstances.

In the end, it is God's Love!

God Wants Your Love

Picture the big game hunter. Always looking to get the "Big Kill." Never stops because he feels there is something out there bigger and better as the ultimate trophy.

That's how passionate God wants our love for Him.

God Loves You.

God's Perfect Love.

There is one that is perfect, Jesus.

But when you think about this, God is perfect. And He made us in His image, so we must be perfect. By God's Love!

Gods "No-Matter" Love

The worst thing a person can do to another is to label or call them names because of their physical and/or mental characteristics. It could harm a person throughout life if they let it. But we only have to answer to one: God. And He doesn't care about all that. It doesn't matter to Him! He made us. God Loves You...just as you are.

God's Personal Love

There are two sides to a person. An outside, this is where we let others know who we are. And an inside, some call it the "darkside." This is where we get to spend time getting to know God. Or, at the very least, allow our intimate relationships in. It's alright to have your fears, or doubts, or deepest secrets, that no one else knows. As long as you let go and let God...Love You!

God Loves a Sinner

We are all sinners. Small or great. Or condemned to Hell.

God loves ALL of us. He made us. And, He gave us the choice to live our lives. In the end...God Loves You!

God Loves You

You are never alone. God is always by your side. GOD LOVES YOU!

Share God's Love

God doesn't want us to keep His love just to ourselves. He wants us to share it with others.

Being kind and compassionate to someone in need. Even a smile to a stranger brightens their day.

Smile, God loves you...and I do too!

This is How God Loves You

For I know the thoughts that I think toward you, saith the LORD, thoughts of peace, and not of evil, to give you an expected end. Jerimiah 29:11 KJV

God wants you to have a good, successful life filled with happiness, because He loves you.

Understanding God's Love

No matter how intelligent the human brain can get, it is virtually impossible even to begin to understand the love God has for you.

That's how much God loves you!

Everything In God's Love

Everything that happens in this world is all in God's perfect timing. It is not for us to understand the reason behind each circumstance. Only to believe and praise God for all things. He does this, because God loves you.

Anytime Praise

We seem to praise God for our success and good fortunes. But we must also praise God during our times of hopelessness and despair. Instead of blaming God for our misfortunes and losses, stand proud and glorify His holy name.

God loves you!

Relationship

Life is not about religion. It is about relationship. A relationship with God. Our savior Jesus Christ. And sharing that relationship with others. Filled with love. God loves you!

God Loves You

It doesn't matter who you are, what you are, what race you are, what ethnicity you are, what culture you are...God loves you just the same. He created you. Share His love. Be yourselves; find harmony and peace with others. Jesus says, "Love one another as He loves you." Peace be with you. God loves you!

God Will Not Abandon You

You are created by God. Nothing...Nothing is impossible for God.

We live in an age of physical, technical, and spiritual advances.

With it also comes hunger, oppression, and depression.

Now added into the mix, world chaos and uncertainty amidst the coronavirus.

This world does not revolve around us, but....belongs to God.

And God will not abandon you. Because God loves you!

God's Validated Love

So many of us are seeking validation from others. Even when they are not publically asking for it. The emotion lingers in our hearts.

God created us. God loves us. That should be all the validation we need.

Try to focus on less of what we think others are saying and thinking of our self-worth in this life. And focus more on why Jesus Christ died on the cross for us.

God loves you!

God Is in Control II

God is in control. GOD! G O D !!!

Not a human being. No one person has the right or privilege to be in control of another human being or beings.

Human trafficking is the worst kind of treatment towards another human being. It's wrong! It's slavery! It's degrading! It is not love. God loves you, and does not want harm to you. But man's pride and lust for money has caused such an atrocity on this earth. And it's up to us, people of love, to change this.

God loves you, and I do too!

God Loves You, Even in Times Of Suffering

As we are in pain, injury, or bed ridden, prayers are being said for us by loved ones, family members, friends, and others. But understand, all prayers do get answered, if you believe and trust God with all your heart.

But this too, understand, everything does happen for a reason. Our suffering may be for someone else's reason. They may be the one in need of God. So send your prayers up for them too.

God loves you.

Jesus is for Everyone

Today our scripture reading was taken from Matthew 15: 18-22. A Canaanite woman cried out to Jesus while he and his disciples were dining as guests at a dignitary's home. She insisted Jesus help her daughter who was possessed with demons. The disciples tried to get rid of her, and Jesus at first ignored her. But at her persistence, Jesus looked up at the woman, and said, "Go, because of your faith, your daughter is healed."

Such faith! This is what God asks of us. To believe and love Him with our whole heart and soul.

It matters not what our religion is, our lifestyle, what our race or culture is. Jesus is for everyone!!

Smile! God loves you!

God's Everlasting Love

There is truth to the bible verse from Matthew 6:6, "but when you pray, go into your closet and pray to the Father secretly, there, you will be rewarded by the Father in secret."

Have you prayed on your knees lately? If so, have you ever noticed even the slightest noise or outside disturbance can disrupt your conversation with God? So it is as Jesus tells us, when you pray openly in the synagogues so all to see, you are doing it for your own self-glory; not for, or with, God. You will be rewarded, but not in the Heavenly sense.

That is why you shut off the television or the radio. Excuse yourself if with others. Go into your own room, alone. And take the time to spend with God. Pray! Have a conversation. But, also, be silent, and just listen to what God is telling you.

There, you will know of His enduring, everlasting Love, for you.

God loves you!

Filled With God's Love

Every human being is made up of coded matter, called DNA. From the time of conception to birth and death. If this is all we relied on to give us life, we would all be like robots. It is the spirit of God that fills us that gives each and every one of us LIFE! Our character, our uniqueness, our love.

It is the choice of the individual how he uses that spirit. Or to replace it with ill intentions.

But it is always God who is always there to fill you with goodness and kindness. Righteous love. Why? Because God loves you!

God Loves You in Any Circumstance

Today's collective intentions and prayers are inspired by scripture, Matthew 24:36, "but of that day and hour knoweth no man, no, not the angels in heaven, only the Father."

From the moment we are conceived in the womb to our passing of this earth, only God knows our time.

During my Earthly father's last breaths, my brother made a comment; who's to say one day you walk out in front of a bus and...then, you're gone.

I didn't quite understand it myself at the time, but I did feel differently about death. I used to feel anger on someone, or God, when someone close to me would pass. But during my father's passing, I felt a peacefulness.

As we prayed for intentions today of family and loved ones, whether they be victims of illness, adversity, or wrongful circumstance; or for those who are praying for them, let us bring praise to God and love Him with our whole heart, soul, and mind for no matter, good or bad our circumstance we happen to be in. For, we do not know when it is our time!

Let us be prepared.

God Loves You!

God's Hungry Love

Have you ever felt hungry? Maybe from fasting, or a missed meal. Some of us choose not to eat, for religious, or cultural reasons. And sadly, some of us don't choose, and die from starvation.

That hunger pain becomes more surreal the more we focus on it. Yet, hunger itself is a state of mind. The true essence of hunger is passion.

It's this passion that God has for you. He has the passion beyond all comprehension to love each and everyone one of us.

It's this passion, this hunger, of love He asks of us! God loves you!

EPILOGUE

Personal acclimations of God's Love

GOD LOVES YOU

God loves you. Because He made you. Your outcome is not a twist of fate. You are not a mistake. Because God made you just as you are. The perfect, the intellect, the dumb, and the paraplegic. It matters none. Because in God's eye you are perfect for Him.

You are not alone, even when there is no one else around. Because you have a room full of God to envelope you. To love you. Feel his embrace; His touch: His healing grace. God loves you in the forever.

God loves you,

and I do too!

GOD WANTS YOU

Be not of this world, nor chained to its ways.

Be not of the laws of man, but be bound by the word of God.

Faith will lead you. Hope will guide you. And Love will bring you home!

WORTHY IS MY GOD

I will praise you when I wake, hold your hand for dear sake. Thank you for my day, as I unwind and begin to lay.

I praise you for the good times, and praise you for my rough times. I praise you for the path you set, the guided journey you have led.

I praise you from the meadows, I praise you from the hills. I praise you from the deserts, my Lord it is your will.

I praise you across the vast seas, and I praise you from the lands foreign to me. I praise you in the calm, I praise you in the storm. And I will praise you when the trumpets sound. For you, I adore.

Because, my God, you are worthy of all my praise.

GOD GIVES CHOICE

God gives us life, and at the beginning offers us His full love, and continues that love to our end. He also gives us the freedom of choice.

He gives us the building blocks of truth and righteousness and love. How we accept His laws and commands are entirely up to us. He gives us that choice. We can be a God lover, a God hater. An Agnostic or an Atheist. Or even stand by the devil's side. It's your choice. But, God is in love with you! He loves you. He loves your soul.

We ascertain from the messages by Jesus in Matthew 5:39 - when slapped on the cheek, offer the other; and again from Matthew 5:44 -love thy enemy….Jesus is conveying how God still loves us no matter how cruel we treat Him. And, gives us that choice to do unto others as he has done unto us. That is his command! To love God with your whole heart, mind and soul. And to love your neighbor as yourself.

Do not be apologetic for being a true christian. Do not hang your head in shame. But, go out with a head held high, and a strong loud voice, and proclaim the Good News of the love of Christ.

God loves you,

And I do too!

GOD MAKES NO MISTAKES

God created and made man. He then created and made woman from man. He distinguished the difference by identifying each one with different reproductive organs for procreation. The male; identified by chromosome XY. And the female; identified by chromosome XX. There are no other types. The bible verse from Jeremiah 1:5, states that God knew you before you were in the womb, and sanctified you at birth. God did not make a mistake identifying you a male or female. For you were already blessed and ordained by God for who you are. God does not make mistakes!

He created a beautiful gift to be incubated in a woman's womb. This conception cannot take place unless the XY and XX chromosomes are united for procreation. Even if one or both, or a forced union chooses not to carry through to full term, or chooses an unwanted birth. It is still God's choice, or I should say His plan of creation for this birth to take place. By us making that choice is telling God HE is the one that made a mistake. God does not make mistakes.

Be happy, love yourself, love God, be comfortable for who you are,and how God formed you. No matter how different emotionally, or physiologically, you may feel, there are only two types of chromosomes. God created you either male, or female. By trying to establish any other definition is saying God made a mistake. God does not make mistakes.

God loves you,
And I do too!

Mother's Day

My message today is a little different. We all know we wouldn't be here if it wasn't for women. God bless each and everyone of them that has brought life into this world. God brought Eve from Adam to benefit man, but man cannot exist without women. So, we need each other to exist.

We go through life and for the most part try to do the best we can. And yes we fail,because we are not perfect.

There are some we call the perfect mother, and some we call the worst mother,and variations of in between. We have to remember, we are all a creation of God. There was no manual put out on how to live life, and certainly not one for being a mother.

The worst we could do is persecute mother's for what or maybe what they haven't done to or for us. They try to love us the best they can. Maybe the stress of having a child was too much, and their hormones can cause irrational thinking. Resorting to ending their own and/or the child's life. Addictions to drugs, alcohol or other mind altering inducements. And, even abandonment.

God bless those mothers that hung in there, and still managed to satisfy their man. And God bless and prayers for all those mothers that had it rough.

Jesus has a soft heart for the widowed and orphaned Dand asked all of us to be their caregiver. Turning of age as an adult doesn't automatically make a child an instant adult. Nor does an orphan stop being an orphan. It's up to all of us to take the orphans and widows under our wing and care for them,because their man is not there to sustain their life.

Our upbringing should not define who we become as an adult. But take what is good and loving. And for those mothers that have suffered subpar parenting, and then raised your own children in a loving, Godly wholesome environment God has graced you with abundance.

God loves you
And I do too

COMMITTED LOVE

When I asked God whom shall I meet before the pearly gates

He said, "son I'm not done with you yet".

You have so much to do saving souls in my name.

But like Adam I sent you a helper, a true believer and lover of the Lord

Before you go you must commit and obey to my teachings and commands, for there is only one way to salvation and the doorway is narrow.

I give you a beautiful earthly angel, and tethered together you each will honor, respect, love and cherish each other for all time.

This is my command to you,"Love one another as I have loved you" "be fruitful in your quest, winning souls"!

To know me is to love me.
I remain with you, I ask the same.
Believe in me and you may ask for anything
For I have loved you now pass it on
My father the gardener,
Raised me like the vine   And you are my branches
To produce good fruit from thine
I obey His every word
As you should mine
And remember when you are hated because of me, I
was hated before time.
For my command is to love.
Love one another
The way I have loved you
Share with each other.

REPENT; FOR THE KINGDOM OF HEAVEN IS YOURS

Today's message is taken from Alma 7:14. To repent and accept Jesus in faith; to be born again and cleansed of sin by being "washed" in baptism for to inherit the kingdom of heaven.

This is true, but at the time of our earthly bodies to expire,our spiritual existence carries over into the spiritual boundaries of life.

Our salvation has been won when God's grace has been offered upon us; when Jesus Christ carried out his mission of dying on the cross for all our sins,so that we may live.

John 15:13 The greatest love a person can show is to die for his friends. Jesus loves you that much as the Father has loved him.

God loves us so much so that it's beyond our human comprehension to understand. And by his will calls us home when it's time,regardless of our time spent on earth. This is why Jesus said in John 15:16, I chose you, you did not choose me...17 This is my command: Love each other!

God loves you
And I do too.

Having Faith and Belief

Our scripture reading today was from Matthew 14 : 22 -33. Jesus walked on the water.

After Jesus dismissed the crowds, he sent the disciples to go across the sea while he went off by himself to pray. Later, the disciples saw a figure walking atop of the sea towards them, and Jesus called out to them. Peter asked Jesus to command him to also walk on the water. And Peter walked on the water to Jesus. But, as the wind blew he became frightened and started to sink. In fear, he cried out to Jesus to save him.

Peter's sudden lack of faith and trust put fear and doubt not only in his mind, but in his spirit. Where he had to call on Jesus to help him.

We can apply this scripture to our daily lives now. Take for instance the Covid-19 scare. Sure, people are getting sick, and dying. But this happens everyday regardless of the Caronavirus.

The world has been put into such a fear of this unseen illness, that it has disrupted our daily lives.

But, God says, trust and believe and love him with your whole heart and soul, and you will achieve anything. Just know, everything you have, everything you do...comes from God.

Another example, a coworker speaks openly of his aches and pains. So it is, he has given the devil the opportunity to cause him to be ill. I speak of goodness and rejoice in what the Lord has given me (even though I struggle with a few internal issues) I do not let others or the devil hear my woes. And my health and continence remains steadfast.

If we do not have faith and belief in God with our whole heart and soul; by having fear and doubt, we give the other one the opportunity to steer our soul, and put God to the side...and we SINK.

Trust in God, Love, and believe in Him. Your world will be happy, joyful, and filled with love, for God, yourself, and others.

God bless you.

God loves you!

The Grass is Always Greener on the Other Side of the Fence

I'm sure you've heard this term before. Life looks like it could be better if only you had a different job, or lived somewhere else, or even had a different family.

You may question, what is the purpose of my life? Or, I just don't know what my goals are, or my calling?

You may seem like what you do is insignificant. Or, maybe, too much going on. And you may not quite understand what it is you should be doing.

But God does! No matter how little or great you are doing in your life, it is all part of God's plan. He uses you to His needs for the love of humanity.

The poor, the rich, the sinners, the saints, hungry or glutten, young and old...God uses all of us. We are His mix.

Are we willing to live by His two commands?! Love God with all your heart, mind and soul. And, Love one another as thine self.

Be happy with yourself. Be happy with what you're doing. Not to worry, or envy your neighbor. Praise God and offer Him the glory for your life.

God bless you!

God loves you!

GOD'S LOVING GRACE

In our times of struggle; in our times of sinning; it has been the grace of God that pulled us through.

When we feel God's love flowing within us, we tend to take His loving grace for granted. But in our daily prayers try to make a conscious effort of admission that we are powerless without God at the center of our existence.

All the works we do in our lives to try and gain access into heaven comes down to one element. The love that God has for each one of us. And His unconditional grace He bestows upon us, regardless of our works.

God Bless You!

God loves you,

and I do too!